Every working actor knows how dif
"perfect monologue". J.P. has creat
actors. "Killer Monologues" is absolutely terrific.

> Helen Rogers
> President, International Model and Talent
> Association

J.P. Pierce is one of the truly most dedicated teachers I
know. In "Killer Monologues", he has compassionately
put his wisdom to the page. Don't cheat yourself - listen
to all of his good advice and do what is necessary to make
your dreams come true.

> Adam Hill
> Acting Coach, Artist-in-Residence
> Wilkes University

J.P. Pierce has my highest respect and trust in every area of
acting and performing.
> Ron Patterson
> Owner, John Robert Powers Schools,
> Worldwide

Excellent book! J.P. makes it easy for the actor to make the
right choice in monologues. Wonderful, practical advice. A
must-read for every actor!

> Debra-Lynn Findon
> Talent Manager
> JDS, Los Angeles

Finally, a book of monologues and advice that understands
that a good monologue is a scene. As in life, our verbal
thoughts come out of conversation. J.P. has written excellent
conversational dialogue!

> Clair Sinnett
> L.A. Casting Director
> Professor, University of California, Irvine

Very well-written! J.P. has created a great collection of appropriate-length monologues that are truly "actable". The performance advice alone is enough reason to buy this book.

> Michael Cushman
> Personal Manager
> President, Conference of Personal Managers

In the 12 years that I have worked with J.P. he has never failed to impress me with his many talents. I am delighted to endorse his latest achievement, "Killer Monologues". A must for all aspiring actors!

> Joan Stephens
> Joan Stephens Television Workshop,
> New York City

"Killer Monologues" is a great tool with good advice for beginning actors.

> Pam Loar
> Agent, Bloom @ Ford Agency
> Beverly Hills, CA

It's important to be prepared when going in for an audition. "Killer Monologues" has excellent monologues and tips to make you prepared.

> Brad Diffley
> Agent
> Beverly Hills, CA

It's the "mentor" of monologue books. Great for anyone! You owe it to yourself to read it.

> Ben Gould
> Television Star
> "Saved By the Bell: The New Class"

Killer

Monologues

Highly Actable Monologues and
Performance Tips to Give
You an Almost Unfair
Advantage in the
Auditioning
Game

J.P. Pierce

Impact Films
14431 Ventura Blvd., Suite 248
Sherman Oaks, CA   91423
(818) 994-7888

Published in Sherman Oaks, California.

Registered with Writer's Guild of America, West   # 705488

For Additional Copies: Contact your bookstore, or
Impact Films (order form on back page)

**This book has an accompanying video!
See order form on back page.**

Library of Congress Catalog Card Number   98-96377

ISBN   1-892553-00-7

Printed in Canada

This book is dedicated to all of my students,
past, present and future.

In the creative process there is the father, the author of the play; the mother, the actor pregnant with the part: and the child, the role to be born.

- Stanislavski

ACKNOWLEDGMENTS

To God,
I am your humble servant, 'cause, "You da Man".

To Andrea,
Your writing and help have made this book a reality.
Vielen Dank, Schätzli. Alles Gute.

To my family,
I count myself lucky to swim in the same gene pool.

To my friends,
Randy, Ray, Les, Julia,
Sharif, Julie, Ashley, and Michael,
Thanks for the love, thanks for the laughs.
It's not that you all had a lot to do with this book,
I just thought you'd enjoy seeing your names in print.

To my acting coaches,
Adam Hill, Ed Claudio,
Richard Thomas, and Joan Stephens,
Thanks for exposing me to a wonderful new world.

To my mentor, Al Onorato,
This world could use a few more of you, my friend.

To Ron Patterson, Patricia Pascucci,
and the gang at John Robert Powers,
A long-standing debt of gratitude.
Thanks for the opportunity to do what I love.

To Helen Rogers and the IMTA,
Your organization is, "Simply the Best."

Art flourishes where there is a sense of adventure.

- Alfred North Whitehead

Foreword

By Al Onorato
Personal Manager
Former Head of Casting for Columbia Pictures

I am privileged to have been associated with J.P. Pierce for a number of years. He is a man of utmost integrity who is as fine a human being as there is in this world. When he asked if I would be good enough to write a quote, I immediately agreed.

J.P.'s understanding and caring for his students make him an outstanding teacher. I first became aware of his monologue writing ability when a student in one of my classes performed a monologue that I had never heard before. It was touching, humorous and new, which immediately aroused my interest. When I found out that it was written by J.P., I was delighted. His full-length screenplays are also outstanding. In "Killer Monologues", J.P. has put together a variety of pieces and given insight rarely seen in both the situations and the characters.

While this book provides helpful suggestions and self-directing ideas, it still allows the actor or actress to bring their own special touch to each piece.

Go forth and create.

- Al Onorato

CONTENTS

The monologues:

Drama

CONTENTS

Comedy

One of my chief regrets during my years in the theatre is that I couldn't sit in the audience and watch me.

- John Barrymore

Preface

Why? Because I saw a need. A great need. After teaching acting for twelve years, I decided that the only way that I was going to get a decent collection of really actable monologues for my students was to do it myself. Most of the monologues in most of the monologue books just weren't good enough. I knew it, my fellow acting coaches knew it, and my students quickly found that out, too. That's not to say that there's not some great stuff out there. It's just hard to find. Great monologues are like gold to an actor. Many actors find a good one, and keep it in their repertoire for years, performing it anytime they need to show off their best work. But like gold, it's the searching that's difficult. The "right" monologue, once found, is easy to perform. It often feels like it performs itself, with seemingly little effort from the performer. When it feels right, you know it.

Singers and dancers have always known how important it is to choose just the right piece to show off their skills. Let's take a lesson from them, and spend a little time picking something that will make us look our best. A strong singer would never get in front of an audience and sing, "Row-Row-Row Your Boat". They may sing it technically perfect, and try to give a certain punch, but it doesn't give them any room to show off. Neither should we, as actors, try to perform a monologue simply because it's a good story. Choose one that is "actable," and will advance your career.

This collection was written mostly for my students, over a period of many years. It should give you more to choose from. I hope that you can use them to further your career and become rich and famous. Just remember to mention my name when you accept your Oscar.

What is the purpose of a monologue?

Monologues are used for many different reasons. Actors work on them in class to develop their technique. For this purpose, almost any piece is acceptable. You can play a role that is for someone who is perhaps very unlike yourself. For instance, a young, teenage, Asian boy can play an old, black woman. If it helps you to reach, stretch and grow as an actor, then go for it.

Another, perhaps more crucial purpose for monologues, is in their use as an audition tool. If an agent, manager, casting director, theatre director or producer wants to see a polished piece of work from an actor, then a monologue is the most obvious and convenient means to show them what you can do. For this purpose, choosing a piece that is appropriate for your age and type is important. Give them an idea of how they might be able to cast you. If you get a chance to audition for a specific role, having a few different monologues ready to go can give you an advantage by selecting the piece most appropriate for the occasion.

At many auditions, you will be given the chance to perform "two contrasting monologues." This can be interpreted in a few different ways. Usually, it means something light, and something a bit heavier. It can mean one drama and one comedy, or one good-guy and one bad-guy. It can even mean one classical and one contemporary. In any case, it's an opportunity to show some of your range. The opportunity to perform two pieces instead of just one, is an honor and a blessing, since most auditions are a bit rushed. Because of these considerations, most of the monologues in this book are short. Many are around one minute. The short pieces are harder to write, and often harder to perform, but if that's all the time you've got . . .

What is my monologue for?

Ask yourself, "What is this monologue going to be used for?". The answer makes a difference in how you choose your piece. Are you trying to interpret the truth in a scene to fulfill the needs of a playwright? Or are you looking for something to get you noticed? If you keep this in mind when you choose, you will most likely choose better.

Here are some possible uses for monologues:

- Performing in an agent's or manager's office.

- Performing for a producer or casting director.

- Performing for your demo tape.

- Performing for a showcase or competition.

- Auditioning for a theatre company.

- Entertaining your family around the campfire.

- Learning your craft in an acting class.

You will notice that all of these, except the last one, are performances. They are for the purpose of impressing the viewer. That is why performing a monologue is different from performing a full-length piece. When you perform a play or act in a film, the purpose is to be a part of telling a good story. You are part of fulfilling the vision of the playwright and director. The story is the important thing. But when performing a monologue, the story has to take a back seat and let you be the star. Its purpose is to show you off. To get you noticed. To make you a star. This doesn't mean you can "overact". Just choose a piece that gives you room to really do something. You don't want to get out there and die. You want to get out there and kill.

So, what makes a killer monologue?

Don't confuse good writing with a good monologue. Monologues, particularly dramatic pieces, need to be "actable", and here is the biggest problem that I have with most other monologue books. Most of the monologues that I found are stories. Many of them are even good, entertaining stories. A character tells about something that has happened. Notice that I said, "something that has happened." Past tense. In other words, the character is telling a story. If the audience likes it, it's probably because the writing was good. They might even like to "hear" it again. But that doesn't do you any good. A good actable monologue is NOT telling a story. Monologues should be <u>watched</u>, not <u>heard</u>. If the main story line is about something that has already happened, then the audience doesn't feel the urgency. They don't feel like something is happening here.

Playwrights put those moments in plays because they need the exposition to more fully develop a character. A nice back-story can really give an audience a better understanding of why a character does what she does, or why she feels what she feels. But again, what works for a playwright in the context of an entire play, doesn't help when you've got a minute or two to "blow them away."

Stanislavsky was apparently the first to point out that for an actor to be alive on stage, he has to actively pursue an objective. A goal. A desired outcome. Every acting teacher and author has a different name for it, but all seem to recognize it's importance. Acting is doing. Being drunk is not acting. Being sad is not acting. Those are states and feelings and don't give you anything to do. But being drunk and doing your best to convince the cop that you're totally sober, now that's acting. Acting is fighting to get what you want. Every scene, every time. If you want to really show off, don't choose a piece where all your character wants is to tell someone something. That's not enough to get the audience into your head and into your performance. So choose something that gives your character something to do. Get the cop to let you off with just a warning. Get the girl to go out with you. Get the boss to give you that raise. Get your best friend to let you cheat off of his math test. Give your character something to fight for and the audience will notice <u>you</u>, because they will be <u>watching</u>, not just listening. Also, let your character be talking to the person who is most involved. If you are telling a friend about a fight you had with your father, that's not nearly as powerful as showing the fight in progress. The first example gets the audience to think about the lines, and the latter makes them worried. They're going to try to get into the head of your character, and that gets them involved.

Your goal then, is to get the audience or viewer not to just think about the scene, but to really feel something. A killer monologue affects the gut more than the head. To affect the viewer in this way, pick a monologue that allows you to go after a more powerful goal. Strong choices make for strong acting. Life and death. Big risks. Outrageous situations. If they gasp, laugh, scream, cry, fall in love or wet their pants, you're doing your job.

A good comedy monologue does not necessarily need to fit the above guidelines. Many of the best comedies tend to match the guidelines perfectly, but there are exceptions. Your job is to get the viewer as involved as possible in your scene. You will tend to show off your acting better if the piece fits the criteria of a character who is actively pursuing an important role with the person most directly involved, even if it's in a comical way. But if you can get the big laughs through any other method, do it. If you are funny, and really getting your audience to laugh out loud, then you must be doing something right. A stand-up comedy routine does not fit the above guidelines for a good monologue, and it won't really show you off as an actor, but anyone who can get us to laugh will be respected and in demand as an entertainer and performer. Many (dare I say most) of today's sitcom performers came out of the stand-up comedy arena. Some of those performers are better actors than others, but they are all working, and are all (arguably) entertaining. Comedy is tough to find and tough to perform, but in my mind, it's a noble and worthwhile effort. There's nothing quite as fun as getting the laughs.

17

How do I start the monologue?

When you perform, the viewers are judging you from the moment that they see you, even if you are walking in, standing in line, waiting for your turn, or warming up. If you are performing on stage, as in a competition or showcase, or for a theatre audition, you've got to practice your entrance and exit. You may choose to enter in character, and perhaps even begin the lines while you are still off-stage. Or you may enter with the air of an opposite character to set-up a surprise opening. Get creative and figure out how you can start off with a unique entrance, or perhaps a clever exit. Use the room and how it's set-up to give you ideas. Use a prop (if allowed) to take you out of the scene. You may choose to exit in character, or to take a classy little bow and exit gracefully, but your entrance and exit are part of the show.

In any case, don't hold up the process with a lot of "personal preparation time." Sooner or later you will recognize that it's unnecessary, and really just another technique to stall getting started. Other people use that "mental warm-up" to try to impress the viewers with "how well-trained and how deep" they are. If you want to impress, be a pro and just get on with it.

Don't try to set-up the scene by describing who you are and the name of the piece (unless that is a requirement in a particular showcase you have entered). You are usually better off by having your first words be the first words of the piece.

Dress in a manner that best befits the occasion. If it's in an agent's office, you certainly are not going to dress in character. I recommend "upscale casual," if that means anything to you. Don't look like you are going to the prom, and don't look like you just finished working on the car. For me, it's usually khakis and a sport coat, or perhaps a black sweater. Your clothes should be simple and not particularly memorable. You are the commodity here. If your are performing in a showcase, or for your demo tape, it may be completely appropriate to be in a full costume. Let the situation determine what you wear.

Who am I talking to?

Take a look at the monologue. Sometimes it's obvious, sometimes not. If it's not clear who you are talking to, you've got some choices. If you change the person who you are talking to, you can change the feel of a piece. You can experiment with how a scene changes depending on who you decide that your character is talking to. Are you talking to a Mafia hit man, or a judge? A wife, or a mistress? The same lines can take on an entirely different feel. Try to pick the imaginary character who is most involved in the scene. If it's a scene about trying to get a raise, don't choose the scene where you are telling your wife that you're going to ask your boss, choose the scene where you are actually asking your boss. Raise the stakes in the scene by choosing the most crucial person to be telling, asking, threatening or begging.

Make sure that you aren't doing a scene that was designed for playing to one specific character, and delivering it with eye contact directly to the entire audience. When your eyes are moving all around, and you appear to be talking to the various viewers of your piece, and the lines indicate that you are having an argument with your mom, the viewers will be confused on which one of them is Mom. An alternate way to do that scene is to pick one member of the audience, and have that be Mom. It's usually best not to choose one of your auditors. Let them just enjoy the performance.

You can also play around with how that imaginary person is situated. Are they seated? Standing? Are you talking to them on the telephone?   Seated across a desk? Maybe your character is speaking directly to an audience, or perhaps you're speaking directly to the audience as yourself, as in a stand-up comedy format. Have they passed away and are now in a coffin? Any one monologue gives you numerous choices.

Be careful not to give your imaginary character movement. Once you have decided where they are, keep them there. If your eyes trace out a moving path, you will confuse your viewers, and they will think that you are talking to another character.

Can I change a monologue?

Heck, yeah! If you don't like to swear, for example, go ahead and edit. The monologues in this book tend to be pretty tame. I'd give them a PG-13 rating at most. But you may run across other pieces that offend you, or you are afraid that they will offend the viewer. It's a judgment call, and only you can be the judge. It helps if you know something about who your audience is, and what their temperaments are. If you have a specific time limit, edit. Don't worry. If it's one of my pieces, I won't be offended. It's good to know whether it's a popular piece from a famous play or movie because if it's well-known and you change the words around, it might not ring true to them.

If you are concerned about copyrights, don't be. When you perform a scene to get an agent, or manager, you are not making money. When you perform a scene for your own demo tape, you are not making money. If you're not engaged in making a profit when you do the scene, you can pretty much not worry about royalties and copyrights. If you perform in a showcase that pays you or the theatre money, then the writer must also be compensated, and that's what royalties are all about. You can even make copies of a few pages of this or any book without worrying about copyright laws, as long as you are not making any money in doing so.

How far can you go? Do you want to really get creative? As long as the resulting scene works for you, I say, go for it. Change a woman's monologue to a man's. Change an adult's to a teen's. Sometimes it works, sometimes not. But don't be afraid to explore what you might be able to do with a scene. A monologue written for one ethnicity may work well when the details are switched to reflect another ethnicity. You can write a portion of a scene on your own and insert it into an existing piece. You can take two or three pieces and blend them together. Only you can decide if it works or not, and that's what rehearsals are for. When in doubt, however, trust the writers and don't get caught up in too many unnecessary changes. Most of us have spent a while getting the piece just right.

How can I connect better?

Props.   If you are in a monologue competition, you may be very limited in your use of props. They may even state that, "No props are allowed." In many of these cases, you can still use something that you wear, such as glasses, a hat, a veil, a belt or tie, ball-point pen, or other such thing as a prop and no one will accuse you of bringing a prop. Under most other circumstances, there are no such restrictions. You can use a telephone, a briefcase, gun, car, food, or anything else that your piece might benefit from. Remember, you are trying to get your audience to believe that you (and they) are really in this imaginary place. Props can help you do that.

Sets.   This probably only applies if you are doing your monologue as a part of a showcase, or if you are taping it to be a part of your demo tape. In these cases, the more that you can do to raise your production value, the more professional the final piece will look. It helps both you and the viewer get a sense of where you are.

Clothing.   As mentioned in the earlier section, what you wear depends upon where you are performing the monologue. If you are taping the piece, or doing it as a part of a showcase, you may choose to dress the part completely to connect you to the scene. This can also add to the overall production value.

A silent partner.   This is usually impossible in a monologue competition because of rules, so you'll probably have to use an imaginary partner on stage with you, or deliver the piece to someone in the audience. It is unlikely that you will have someone else come along to an agent's office. In this case, there may be several people viewing your performance, and you choose someone there to speak to. For demos and showcases, have that person there and in the appropriate attire. It will help you tremendously in connecting with the scene, and makes immediate sense to the audience.

21

What is a soliloquy?

A soliloquy is a monologue that a character says to himself. It may be done alone, or when unaware of the presence of other characters. Hamlet's , "To be, or not to be..." is perhaps the most famous soliloquy. Although it's a great moment in "Hamlet", soliloquies are a class of monologues that I don't recommend for audition purposes. When you speak alone on stage, or you are doing a "thinking out loud" type of monologue, you are doing just that. There are a couple of problems with this. First, you are just thinking out loud. That doesn't give you much chance to fight for something that you want. If you are not strongly pursuing an objective, you're not acting. Otherwise, it's a recital. Second, since most of us don't think out loud in that way, it seems unnatural for the audience to watch someone do it. It almost always appears contrived. If you find a piece that appears to be a soliloquy, remember to talk to someone.

Should I try writing my own monologue?

A lot of actors want to try this. If you are one who wants to create your own piece, I say give it a try. You've got nothing to lose. But I will also caution you that when you get your chance to impress an agent or manager, or if you are competing before a panel of important industry people, you should probably trust the work of those who write plays, screenplays and monologues often. Caution: many self-written monologues tend to become very self-indulgent.

If you want to find something that hasn't been done too often, you might find it possible to change one of your favorite dialogues into a monologue by condensing two character's lines into one. This doesn't always work, of course, but you might run across some that work very well this way. Experiment in rehearsals, at home or in acting class, and see what kind of response you get.

How can I make my monologue performance more powerful?

Sorry, there's no sure formula here, but I can give you some guidelines that may help to answer your question. The primary thing to keep in mind is to view the whole piece from the audience's perspective. Once you've analyzed a monologue and you've gotten an idea of it's potential, close your eyes and think about how it might look it you were watching from "out there." Run the movie projector in your head and try to visualize the entire piece, from entrance to exit. What can you do that has boldness in it? What can you do that adds an unexpected moment? The reason that it's impossible to say, is that it must be specific to the monologue, to the room you'll be performing in, the type of audience who will be viewing your performance, and most importantly, it is specific to you. What can you do that will make your performance be remembered? What rules or standards can you break? I've had students begin sitting in a chair with their backs to the audience. Others started their piece while sitting in the audience, and others in a competition spoke directly to the person who was there to keep track of time. There have been countless other choices, and most have worked, some better than others. The point is to have enough guts to take some risks.

Another point to keep in mind, especially with the "heavier" dramas, is not to "fall into the trap." That means, not to play the obvious emotions of a scene. Remember, you don't act emotions, you act actions. The emotions will be there when you forget about them. When you pour yourself into fighting to get what your character wants in the scene, the emotions will grab ahold of you, and you've just got to let that happen. If it's a sad monologue, don't play a sad character. The audience will usually feel that pain a lot more if you look for the opposite. Explore playing a sad piece with as much hope and glory as possible. The sadness won't be felt by you, but your audience may weep. You can manipulate the audience. You've got that power. Don't you love it?

23

Everybody wants to be Cary Grant.
Even I want to be Cary Grant.

- Cary Grant (1904-1986)

The Monologues

America is my home now.

Drama.

Best suited for: Male or female, various ethnicities.

Change the ethnicity and sex to suit your needs. You may choose to be talking to an INS official, or someone else who would hold this kind of power over you. You don't want to go back, so fight hard to stay, being careful not to lose your temper.

You want to send me back to [Estonia]? But I have lived in America for almost three years. I have my friends here, my job......everything. I cannot go back, Sir. You don't know how it is there. So different. So hard to have a happy life. I came to America with so many hopes and dreams and a lot of them came true. So, my marriage to the American [woman] didn't work out. That should not force me to lose my right to be here. You don't want to send me back. It would be like punishing me for a failed marriage. I have been a good worker, Sir. Always came on time. Never missed a day. I was never involved in anything illegal. I'm a good and honest person. Better than many of your citizens. I clean up after them. I empty the trash-cans in your big glass buildings. Just let me continue doing that, Sir. Please. Don't send me back. I wouldn't know how to start all over again. America is my home now.

Another woman.

Drama.

Best suited for: Female, late 20's and up.

You may choose to play the "bad guy" here, but you've still got to justify your position. You would not behave this way unless you truly believed that you have been treated unfairly by your man and his daughter. You don't feel like you are being unreasonable. Stand up for yourself, and get the attention and appreciation that you deserve.

No. Absolutely not. If your daughter wants to play with a computer then take her to the store and buy her one, but she can't use mine anymore.

You know, every weekend when she comes and stays with us, I feel like the fifth wheel on a car. The way you look at her and spoil her and the way she looks at me when she sees how hurt I am to be left out and somehow not important to you anymore.

You two are such a team. You've got all your cute, little secrets. I hear you whisper and giggle while I cook her favorite dish, which of course never tastes as good as her mother's.

Your "little angel" can be a real little devil when you're not around, and I feel my hands are tied because you made it clear that she is going to have the time of her life when she's with us.

Well, you have another woman in your life now, and if you don't start backing me up, making her show me more respect and explaining to her that I am going to become a part of your team, then I won't interfere. I'll stay out of your way . . . forever.

Come here.

Drama.

Best suited for: **Male, late teens and up.**

This is the most frightening short monologue I've seen on stage. Try beginning with a certain amount of anger. This guy just hit Jessica, after all. The piece is very simple in story, but it's in the delivery that it comes alive. That's what makes this such a powerful scene to watch. (Hint - try luring your audience into a sense of safety by chuckling softly to yourself just before you scream out the final, "Come here.")

Dammit, Jessica!! Why do you make me do that! I told you to have this place cleaned up when I got home. How come it's still such a mess? . . . Huh? . . . Why is it still such a mess?!!

Look, Honey, I'm sorry. It's been a tough day. Come here. . . . Come here. . . . . Come here. . . . **COME HERE**!!!!

(He quickly removes his belt and holds it ready to deliver a severe blow) You know, I am sick and tired of your disrespect! . . . No. Forget it. You're not worth going to jail for again. (He exits.)

Don't cry now, Billy.

Drama.

Best suited for: Female, any age.

Once in a while, a good piece comes along that is not particularly dynamic. This one doesn't leave much to fight for, but it still seems to work well for touching our hearts. I think that it works particularly well for a girl to be talking to her brother, but you can find lots of other possibilities. If you can do this with Billy present, as in a showcase or a demo tape, it can add a lot to the audiences gut-level response.

The test came out positive, Billy. Our prayers have been answered. I can give you my kidney, and it's a perfect match. "Good compatibility," the doctors say. No more hooking you up to this machine every day....., we can finally go on vacation to that island in the Caribbean you always talked about.

Don't cry now, Billy. You are going to be healthy again. I'm going to give you a damn fine kidney. Man, how thankful I am for my healthy living. And you have to take care of this kidney, Billy. I think you should even become a vegetarian, too. You know it's just not used to dealing with all that saturated fat.

We'll both be just fine, Billy. Everything is going to be fine.

Don't make a big mistake.

Drama.

Best suited for: **Chinese male, 40 and up. Easily converted for females, and for other ethnicities.**

This has a high level of importance because of the father's love for his son. It also has a high level of urgency because of the time element of the upcoming events. Don't let him blow it. Use every bit of persuasion you've got, and this piece can really be touching.

Wait, wait, wait, wait. Wait a minute. It <u>is</u> my business! Son, you are my only child. You know, the whole family, aunts and uncles, are all against the idea of you getting involved with this woman.

First of all, you are Chinese. But Julia is a foreigner! If your mom were here today, do you know how she would feel? She would be horrified!

Son, don't you want to have children of your own, someday? Think about it, you are only twenty-one, and still in college. She is almost twice your age! When you reach forty, she'll be sixty!!

(Then several frustrated sentences in Chinese to himself.)
Think about your future, son! Of course, it's your future, and your life. I love you, son.

Give him a chance.

Drama.

Best suited for: Female, late teens and up.

If you didn't love your mom very much, you'd never have this conversation. So don't let this become snide and defensive. Fight to get her to see that she needs to open up her heart. Your passion for her love and approval has to show, or else this will come across as bitter. Show her your love.

So it is his skin color. Well, excuse me, Mother. Don't give me that look. You said that my happiness is all that counts. You said, "whatever makes you happy makes me happy too." So, now I am happy. More than ever. So where is your joy, your smile, the hugs and everything?

Are you really so narrow-minded that his being black troubles you? You know of all the mothers in the world, I expected you to be different. I expected you to be open, tolerant, broad-thinking and modern. But now you are giving me that look and the, "only-in-your-best-interest" crap. I don't wanna hear it, Mother. None of it. I'm happy. Really, truly happy and I want to share this with you. So come on, smile, hug me and give him and yourself a chance. I know you'll love him and one day you'll be sorry for not having him let into your heart sooner.

Guilty of being a jerk.

Drama.

Best suited for: **Male or female.
20's to 50's.**

You need only be of reasonable age to be cast as a lawyer to play this role. Courtroom dramas usually give a clear objective to the piece; to win the case. Fight to win the trust of the jury, so that they see things your way.

Ladies and Gentlemen of the jury. Our purpose here today is to determine the future of this man, Daniel C. Trudeau. Freedom or Prison. To determine his future we've taken a long hard look at an event in the past. Last year on the night of Jan. 12th, a woman was murdered. This man's wife, Margaret A. Trudeau was shot twice at close range. We all know that. You've heard in this court that Daniel and Margaret used to fight a lot. That Daniel was known to raise his voice. That he even hit her on a few occasions when he came home drunk. Do I think he's guilty? Yeah. I think he's guilty of being a total jerk. But he did not murder anyone. He never even owned a gun. This murder was planned. Not some argument that got out of control. Mister Trudeau loved his wife. Somebody deserves to pay for this with their life. But I say, we've got the wrong guy.

Happy Birthday, Felipe.

Drama.

Best suited for: Female, 40 and up, Spanish-speaking.

If you have the ability to speak well in a foreign language, a monologue can be a good way to show that ability. Play this scene in any way that strikes you. It can be done as though you are speaking to a grave-site, to his spirit, to his photograph, or anything else that you can think up. Be careful about playing this too sad. She is obviously a proud woman, and although this can be a sentimental piece, she's strong and perhaps still a bit angry, even after all this time.

It's been twelve years, Felipe. Twelve years. Do you know how much you hurt me when you left? *Aún, no lo puedo creer. Aún, no te he perdonado.* I still haven't forgiven you.

I have brought up your daughters into fine young women. I have raised your son into a courageous and thoughtful young man. You should be proud. But what you did to me twelve years ago; your carelessness, your foolishness; it cost you your life, and it cost me my husband.

But there is one thing that I can count on. *Hay algo con lo que sí puedo contar. Algo que sí es seguro.* You can't let me down like that again . . . because you can only die once.

Anyway, *Feliz Cumpleaños,* Felipe. Happy Birthday.

He said my name.

Drama.

Best suited for: **Female, late 20's and up.**

This piece is purely the telling of a story. It doesn't give you, the actor, a lot of room to show-off, but enough of the time, if you can get the audience to feel something, you will get the credit for a great performance. In other words, this piece is fairly easy to do. Make sure that you are happy and excited in your recollection. The sadness should be held entirely by the audience, not by your character.

Yesterday was the first time Tommy said my name. He opened up his big blue eyes, looked at me, smiled, and said my name. I was so overwhelmed to finally hear him talk. He looks so vulnerable, so lost in his pajamas laying in that big bed.

I made him mashed potatoes with gravy and lots of extra butter. His favorite. Later, I sang him his lullabies and told him the story about Nesto, the Dachshund that rescues a little boy. He adores that story. It always makes him giggle and cry at the same time. When I leave his room, I always make sure the little light in the corner is on. Usually he falls asleep within a few minutes. He needs his sleep. Eight or nine hours, at least. He takes lots of naps during the day, which is good for him.

Sometimes he wakes at night. Then I'll bring him a hot cocoa and show him some pictures of him, me....us. He loves the ones of our honeymoon in Germany and always wants to see the ones of David, our first son.

Yeah, it sure feels good to hear him say my name again.

I blew it. I'm sorry.

Drama.

Best suited for: **Male, 25 and up**.

When you're guilty, you're guilty. Do your best to make your sin seem as insignificant as possible. Allow a range of emotions to come over you, after all, you're not such a bad guy, are you? While you admit your guilt, you don't feel that you deserve to be treated like this.

Honey, she doesn't mean anything to me. You're the one I married. You're the one I love. Not Janice.

So I messed up. So what? So it was your best friend. So what? Would you rather it be with someone you don't know, or some stranger? Someone who could have a disease or something?

I'm sorry. Look, if it means anything, I was thinking about you when I was with her. That's got to mean something, right? Would you rather that I was thinking of her while I was with you?

Okay. Wait a minute. I realize that I'm saying some incredibly stupid stuff here. If you could stop packing up my things, then maybe this wouldn't be so difficult! Look, I'm a guy and I messed up and I'm sorry. Please stop packing my stuff. Stop it . . . stop it . . . stop it, stop it, stop it, STOP IT, STOP IT, **STOP IT**!

No. Forget it. Go ahead. Go ahead and pack all my stuff. Put all my socks in there. I don't need you. Do you think Janice was the only one? She wasn't the first, and she won't be the last. I can get plenty of women to cook for me. I can get plenty of women to clean for me. I can get plenty of women to be good to me. I'll just go. . . I'll just go . . . to . . .

Look. I said that I was sorry, okay? I'd rather stay with you, and it will never ever happen again. I swear. Besides, you need me around. Who's gonna show Johnny how to throw a curve ball? Who's gonna teach Jason how to bait a hook? And Akurri is still a puppy. Who's gonna train him how to do all those tricks that the kids love. And you. You need a man. A real man to help out and take care of things. I'll be better. I promise. Just don't make me leave.

45

I finally have peace.

Drama.

Best suited for: **Female, 20's and up.**

Decide on a motive when delivering this (or any) piece. You are probably trying to get a light sentence from the judge. If doing this in front of a live audience, remember to focus on the judge in a fixed place, and keep your eyes coming back to that place when you make an important point. You might also pick a single member of the audience to be the judge.

I know I'm guilty your Honor. Yes, I took that knife and stabbed it into his heart. I know I had no right to take justice into my hands, but he started to hurt my babies again, your Honor. My beautiful, innocent children. Who could do something like that? If he had continued to beat me up.....you know, I could deal with that. I dealt with it the last seven years. But I told him, "Not the children." "Not the babies, Russell."

I threatened to leave him, but he told me he would find me, no matter what, no matter where. I knew he was right. I knew I couldn't just leave and go away. Russell would have found me. He told me so. I believed him. When I took that knife I knew I might go to jail for it, but I had no choice. For the first time in seven years, I can wake up in the morning without having fear. I can come home after work without worrying if he's been to the kid's rooms. I don't need to be afraid of him coming home drunk at night, ready for what he called, "The wild bedroom battle." No more do I need to push myself between him and my children, and no longer do they need to see their mother with a bruised face. Now I have peace, your Honor. I finally have peace.

I need to be with my kids.

Drama.

Best suited for: Male, late 20's and up.

Perhaps there's nothing that we will fight harder for than our own kids. Most parents would sacrifice their own life for their children. You got a bum deal on the custody, and you've got to try a gentler approach to try to get your kids back. The first line tells you that this is a phone monologue, which tend to work well because the audience is used to not hearing the other side of a conversation when someone is on the phone. By the end, it's clear that this approach is not working. Your response can give us a hint on what happens next.

No, Monica, please don't hang-up on me. I really need to talk with you . . . No, no lawyers this time. I want to talk with you. I want to talk about our children. Come on, Monica, we used to be a family once. We were married for ten years for God's sake. Why do we suddenly need lawyers to talk about something?

Okay, okay I'll make it short . . . the reason I'm calling is because I'm not happy with the one-weekend-a-month deal. It's just not enough, Monica. You know how much I love those kids, I cannot be without them for such a long time. I simply need to see them more often. I miss them so much. I do nothing but count the days 'til I'm with them again. The daily habits . . . you know, driving them to school in the mornings, playing sports with them in the backyard and telling them my crazy little monster stories in the evening. I just need more time with them, Monica. Please!! Monica? Monica? Are you there? Monica!

I want us to be a family.

Drama.

Best suited for: **Male or female, 20's or younger (possibly older).**

This is a straightforward struggle to get your dad to stay. It gives your character a lot to fight for, so fight!

Dad? Can I talk to you for a minute? I just want to say a few things. I don't know exactly what's going on here. But I know the statistics are against us. Maybe you and Mom don't get along. Maybe you've been together so long that you've forgotten that you love each other. Maybe you've met someone new and you think she's going to keep you young and you'll be happy. Or maybe it's me. If it's me, Dad, I'll try harder. I will! I'll be a good [son] and I'll make something out of myself and you'll be proud. You'll say, "Hey look, that's my [son]."

Don't leave, Dad. Please. I need you. Mom and Lauren need you. Don't split us up. I want us to be a family. Not a statistic.

I will fight like ten lions.

Drama.

Best suited for: **Male, teens.**

You've got nothing left to live for, but to avenge the deaths of your family. The time for the rites of manhood has been thrown upon you. The age of innocence is past. Only by demanding will you be taken seriously by this military leader. Stand up to this powerful man, and show him that you are tougher than you appear. Give him every reason to say, "Yes."

Hear me, Captain. I demand that you listen to me. You bring me back the bodies of my father and brothers and expect me to just stay behind here and mourn? I am not an old village woman, Captain. I must be given the chance to avenge their deaths. I must be allowed to fight with you against those who did this. I know you see me as too young. You would even call me a boy. But with the hatred that burns in me, I will fight like ten lions. I know many will die, and I know I may be one of them. The way I see it, if this "boy" doesn't get a chance to fight, his life as a man won't be much worth living. Please, Captain, let me join you.

I'm in there.

Drama.

Best suited for: Male or female, all ages.

"Wow." That's what most people have said when they saw this monologue done well. It has won numerous awards for those who have done it. It's risky, it's controversial, and it can only be used in certain situations.

Portraying a handicapped person can be done really well, or can be done really badly. There's not much middle ground. Study the movements, speech and posture. When you drop the characterization, show a bold and powerful character underneath, and don't hold back.

(With full handicap, from the first time we see this character.)

There once was a boy who felt their pain, he had a life but had no name.

(Getting very flustered, turns for help) I can't. I can't do it.

(Then, building up enough courage, talks directly to the audience, no longer doing the monologue). I look at you. I know what you see when you look at me. I know. But do you know what's inside? Do you know what you'd see if you'd just look deeper? . . . Do you?!

(Steps to side, takes glasses off, drops all handicaps). This. I'm in there. I've always been in there, and that's where I'll always be. You've got a little vision trouble there, don't you. Myopia. Near-sightedness. Well, fight it! Look deeper! I wouldn't want you to miss out on a really cool person. (Steps back to side, glasses back on, regains handicaps.) And when the people passed him by, they listened close and heard him cry.

It's not his problem.

Drama.

Best suited for: **Male or female, any age.**

Here's a short monologue that can really pluck the heartstrings. In trying to get the most from this piece, watch out that it doesn't become too heavy. Look for the opposite, and perhaps play this as a wonderful and happy relating of a personal experience. Although this piece does not directly involve the person being spoken to in the script, it's an opportunity to show a very tender side.

Having a severely handicapped brother can be pretty difficult for me to handle sometimes. I mean, my friends don't want to go places with us because they're too embarrassed to be seen with him. And people think he's stupid because he doesn't walk, and talk, and look like they do. He's a lot smarter than they'll ever know. It's not his fault he was born like that.

Ya know, no matter what we do together, we always end up having fun. And when he smiles and drools at me, that's how he tells me he loves me.

Ya know what? (long pause) It was never really his handicap, it was mine.

Just like me.

Drama.

Best suited for: **Male or female, teens to perhaps late 20s**.

This piece is specific for showcase scenarios, but may be one that you can work into something for your needs. It can have a really creepy feeling to it when the audience catches on to how naive this person is. It tends to work well when you play it excited and hopeful. When performing a monologue, you should never worry about what the audience is thinking (stay tuned-in to the circumstances of the story and fight to accomplish your goal). In rehearsing, however, think about how you can make choices about this piece to make the audience want to jump up and shout, "Don't be such an idiot!".

I was going to do my monologue for you, but I guess that I don't need to compete anymore. The reason that I came here was to try to get an agent, and I just talked to one out there in the hall, and guess what? He likes me! He invited me to come up to his hotel room tonight at eleven. He said it would be just the two of us and we could really talk better then. I know that's kinda late, but agents are busy people, right?

I do have a curfew at ten, but this is a once-in-a-lifetime opportunity and I'm not about to blow it. I'm just so excited, I can't believe it! He didn't say exactly why he wanted me to meet him in his room, but I guess it's to sign contracts, right? He did say he'd order up a bottle of champagne for a celebration toast.

Now, the reason I came up here is because I want you to get to where I am. I know that I've looked forward to this for a long time, and I'll never forget this night. If you work hard, stay focused on your goal, and use your instincts like I have, someday you'll be in my position. Good luck!

Let me keep my baby.

Drama.

Best suited for: **Chinese female, late teens to early 30's.**

There are some monologues that are very specific in terms of who can realistically play them. Here's one. Perhaps it can work with other ethnic groups, but it's up to you to see if that works or not.

The idea here is that you are begging your husband's parents not to send your child away. You've got a lot to fight for in this scene. The Chinese language can be used to change mood when you see that the respectful approach isn't working. Go ahead and vent. But be cautious. These parents-in-law are the ones with the power.

Gong-gong, Po-po, I know that you wanted a grandson to carry on the family name, but Chinese law allows for only one child, and I want to keep my baby. I can't bear to give up my own daughter. Every time I hold her close to me and feel her warmth and listen to her heartbeat, I think . . . this is the precious child that came from inside of me. She's so beautiful. Don't you want to see her? Look, Po-po, she has your eyes. And her smile, Gong-gong, she smiles just like you . . . *Ne men tai may yo ren shin bi wo bu yao ze ji de hai ze! Cho ni bu yao bi wo fang chi wo de nu er!*

Please. . . Don't make me give up my baby.

Life will be so much better.

Drama.

Best suited for: **Male, late 20's and up.**

This is a piece about desperation. It might sound like a crazy idea to you (I hope it does), but people do this stuff every day. Make a clear case to your wife. Show her that you are sincere, and try to make her see the sense in your idea.

Why? Because I've got to. I've got to at least try. Honey, I've had my job for six years. Six years. I'm not moving up. I'm an elementary school teacher and that's it. There's no future for me there. Those students don't respect me. Of course not. If I were them, I wouldn't respect me either. It's just not in my blood.

Now, I know you're not going to like this idea, so I'm just going to come right out and say it. I'm going to produce movies. Wait, wait, wait. Don't say anything, okay? Just hear me out. Now I know I'm smart and I learn fast and I know I can do it. Besides, you always said you liked my comments about how actors did in movies. And I'm great at movie trivia. Honey, I'm serious about this. We sell our furniture, quit our jobs, move to LA as soon as possible and start making movies. We've got about twenty thousand in our savings and retirement funds that I can use to buy whatever equipment I'll need. Don't worry, the first money I make back, will replace our savings, I promise. Life will be so much better, and we'll celebrate together. Come on, Honey. If you believe in me, you'll say yes. If you don't believe in me, then I guess that answers my question in a different way. Well, what do you say?

Like a vacation, almost.

Drama.

Best suited for: **Male,
20's and up.**

One of the more creepy monologues I've seen. Your job is to get Thomas to say, "Okay" to this crazy, doomed scheme. You may not be very confident. After all, you're in big trouble. But make it sound like everything is cool, and nothing could go wrong. Although written here as a phone monologue, it may be easily converted for a face-to-face meeting, if you prefer.

Hello, Thomas? It's Larry. Uh, I'm in a bit of trouble and I need your help. Let's see, I guess I'd better start at the beginning. I've got a little bit of a gambling thing. A habit I guess you'd say. I mean it's not usually a problem, I often do pretty well. But things have gotten.....sorta out-of-control lately, I don't know. Anyway, listen, there's these guys. I owe 'em a lot of money. Money I don't have. And these guys, Thomas, they, uh...., they take this stuff rather seriously. They want me to drive a car for them. One trip. A station wagon, down to Hermosillo, Mexico, and back. They didn't say why or what's in the car or anything, but....they said it would look a lot better if I was driving with my family. I told 'em I don't have a family and they said, "Get one."

Thomas, I know that this is totally safe. Really, there's nothing to worry about. Helen and Jimmy would just be gone overnight with me. It would be like a vacation almost. I hear it's a beautiful country, and we'd sing songs and stuff. I'm sure everything will go smoothly. Thomas... if this wasn't really important to me.... I wouldn't ask.

Marco.

Drama.

Best suited for: Male or female, teens and up.

Perhaps this piece looks short, but silence can be golden. It was written to be almost exactly one minute in length, with plenty of room for pauses. I suggest not raising your voice, nor showing too much sarcasm. If you really are the one in control, you don't need to yell. This piece becomes extra powerful when done very calmly, but with focused intensity. You decide just who Marco is. Perhaps a gang leader, an abusive ex-boyfriend, or step-father.

Oh, yes. This is the point where I'm supposed to be afraid. You want me to be afraid, Marco? . . . . Oooh. . . . . I'm not the [girl] you used to know, Marco. I'm different now. I've grown up. And I can see right through all your lies and all the crap that seems to somehow intimidate the others. But there's one truth that I know without any doubt. Believe this. If you ever even try to touch me or my sister again . . . . I'll kill you.

My sister deserves better.

Drama.

Best suited for: **Male or female, 20's and up.
(Easily converted for younger).**

Torn between family and friend, you discover that blood is thicker than water. Friendship might keep you from blowing up at Jack, but you will protect your sister at all cost.

My sister deserves better, Jack. And better is what she's going to get.

Kathy told me several weeks ago that you've been drinking a lot lately, and treating her like [dirt]. You and I have been friends a long time, so I decided to stay out of it. But last night I saw you at the Pegasus club with that short redhead, and our friendship is about to come to a screeching halt.

Kathy is my only sister, Jack, and I would do anything in her best interest. You've got a few possible choices here. For the time being, in honor of our friendship, I won't say anything about the redhead. But either make it right with Kathy, or let her go. 'Cause if you don't do something about it . . . I will.

No monsters.

Drama.

Best suited for: **Male or female, 20's and up.**

Fight, don't beg.   In this courtroom drama, you're not fighting to prove guilt.   You are fighting for maximum penalty.   For real justice in your character's eyes.   Without this execution, you will feel no sense of closure.

When I was very little, my mother would tuck me into bed and if she thought I was scared she would reassure me by saying that there are no ghosts and no monsters. No ghosts and no monsters. I used to believe that.

She doesn't say that anymore, your Honor. She doesn't say anything anymore because a real-life monster, that man (points), Jeffrey Blaine Williams, broke into her home 16 months ago and killed her, just like he had done to seven others prior to being caught. There has never been any doubt about his guilt.

Please, your Honor, I beg you to reconsider your judgment to grant a stay of execution. A life prison sentence is not enough. We've got to eliminate this monster, so that I, and the ghost of my mother, can again rest easily at night.

Now you're gone.

Drama.

Best suited for: Male or female, any age (especially teens).

Don't let the fact that the person you are talking to is dead stop you from making your point.   You loved [her], and until now, you never told [her].   Speak now or forever hold your peace.

God, I can't believe it, just last week we were talking. I told you not to get into the car with that guy! He was such a jerk! I miss you so much. Remember the time when we were at the beach with all our friends? We all got into a huge water fight. It was so fun! When I saw you laughing and having a good time, I realized then how much I loved you.

I'm so mad at myself! I had so many chances to tell you! Now you're gone and you will never know. I hate myself for that. I don't think I'll ever meet anyone quite like you. You were such a good friend. You always made me feel good. Well, I guess I'd better get going. I will never forget you and I will always love you.

Power.

Drama.

Best suited for: Teenage male.

Sincerely tough or "wanna-be" tough. This monologue is more about imposing your will and flexing your power of intimidation than it is about what you're asking for. Know that Ricky is afraid, and enjoy tormenting him. As long as you've got your gun, this guy is no more than a dog to you.

Yo, Ricky! Where's my money? Wait a minute, don't bother answering that 'cause I know you don't got it. But I know somethin' else, too. I know you're gonna get it. How do I know? Do you know why a punk teenager like me can mess with a thirty-somethin' year old dude like you? (He points to the inside of his jacket, showing his gun to Ricky.) Power. That's why I'm packin' twenty-four/seven. I could smoke you right here, right now. I could wax your whole family in the middle of the night.

You want a happy ending to this story, Ricky? . . . Huh?! . . . Bring me my three G's by Saturday, and we'll all sleep better at night.

She smiled.

Drama.

Best suited for: **Male, any age.**

The person that you are talking to is going through something similar to what you went through. Comfort them. Make them see that bad things happen, but we can still move on. Otherwise, this becomes the simple telling of a personal story. The telling of a story has to come with a reason so that you've got something to <u>act</u> with.

By the time I got there, it was all over. Renee and I went as soon as we got the news. When we arrived at the hospital, Mom came out and when she saw us, she smiled. Her smile was warm and friendly and caring. But I knew right away what it meant. I knew that the smile was there to give me strength. To help make it seem okay. To prepare me. But knowing what that smile was there for made it . . . ominous. It was a message I'll never forget. It meant my dad was gone.

He was a great dad and he lived a long and happy life. Mom and Renee took it so well. They were both so strong. I think women in general are better about that kind of stuff. I remember feeling very selfish, because, my dad and I had had our time together. I just wanted more.

Sixty Seconds.

Drama.

Best suited for: **Female,
late teens and up. (Eastern
European accent preferred.)**

If you look the part, and can pull off a decent Russian accent, you might try this one, but it's a great choice if you've already got the accent.

Fight to get this guy to join you. You've tried everything. Now you've got to give him an ultimatum. You can answer the question, "Does he, or doesn't he?" by your choice of exit, or you may choose to leave us hanging.

You have sixty seconds, Mikhail Semyonovich! Sixty seconds to explain to me why you lost your nerve. (pause) Why do you sit silent when it is time for us to run?

Perhaps you have reconsidered the advice of your comrades? Perhaps you have forgotten what happened in Petropavlovsk. And Minsk. And Kiev. Well I have not forgotten! The memories and the injustice burn in me like a furnace. I will not stay out here and freeze with you. My rage will keep me warm enough to reach Bratislava, and eventually Vienna.

Your time is up, Mikhail. Join me now....or wish me good luck.

So, you're nothing.

Drama.

Best suited for: **Male or female, Caucasian.**

This monologue is a bit dangerous, but that danger is something that can make a monologue great. Whether you agree or disagree with this character's point-of-view is not important. Simply understand where this person is coming from, just as you would any character that you play. This person probably has a lot of conviction behind his actions. This may be done in the form of a speech to a crowd, to a TV talk show host, to angered parents, etc.

A lot of people ask me why. Why am I doing this? What's the point? I guess it's to make a statement. This campus has an African-American club. There's an Asian club, the Polynesian club, "Nosotros Latinos" and an Arab club. There's even a gay and lesbian club here on campus for those who are so inclined. Now hear me on this, I think that's great. I think that having all those clubs is part of what makes this country a great place to live. Freedom of assembly.

I went in to the Associated Students Union and was able to get before a board of directors. I told them that I wanted to start a new club, so that I could be around people like myself. They asked, "Are you a foreigner?" I said, "No." They asked, "Are you representing a political party?" I said, "No." They asked if I was gay. I said, "No." "So, you're nothing?" they asked. "Nothing?" I said, "No. I'm white." I said I wanted to start a club for white people so that we can be proud of who we are, too. Of course, they said "No." It sounded racist to them. There are seven other clubs on campus based on race and no one questions their motives. But if it's white, it sounds to them like the KKK or something. We're not a hate group. We're not a white supremacy group. But in a land of rich cultural diversity, I just got tired of being . . . "nothing."

Stay.

Drama.

Best suited for: Female, late teens and up.

You've got a powerful goal here; to keep your man alive. He is so enraged that it's going to take every bit of persuasive power that you have to keep him from going after the bad guys. He's brave, but foolish. Knock him off of his white horse before he gets killed. It won't be easy, so fight hard to get him to agree.

No, Kevin, don't go. Please. I don't want to lose you. I know you're mad, and I know you want revenge, but you're not thinking clearly right now and you're going to get yourself killed.

You don't help me if you go out there trying to undo something that has already been done. I have been raped, yes, but it has already happened. We need to face today and tomorrow and I need you for that right here by my side. Strong and supportive to help me get back on my feet so we can carry on with our lives.

I would love to see those guys punished for their crime. I want them sent to the electric chair. But you taking your gang and going out to get revenge, that's not going to do anything good for us. You'll end up dead or in prison. If you really want to impress me, stay.

Steven.

Drama.

Best suited for: **Male (easily converted to female), any age.**

Steven (or a girl, if you choose) is mentally retarded. He has the ability to break the ice and make friends, which is his goal here. You can really go for the heartstrings with this one.

My name is Steven. I play the harmonica. What's your name? . . .That's okay, you don't have to talk if you don't want to. You look afraid. You shouldn't be afraid. They're nice here. They talk nice and give you things to do and the food is good. I've been here for six years. They know me pretty good. The last place I was in had bad food, and sometimes they yelled. I didn't like it.

You see that guy over there? That's Bart. It's short for Bartholomew. He's cool. He's really funny and he calls me his friend. He works on Friday nights and all day on Saturday and Sunday, 'cause he goes to college.

You've got a pretty flower on your coat, so I'll call you Flower, so you won't have to talk until you're ready. Come on, Flower, I'll introduce you to Bart, then you'll have two friends.

Te estoy rogando.
(I'm begging you.)

Drama.

Best suited for: **Hispanic female, late teens and up.**

As with the other monologues that are written specifically for one particular ethnicity, you may be able to make it work for you if it can be done logically. In this piece, use the Spanish lines to vent your frustration in "your native tongue." Get Miguel off of his butt, or you've got to go alone.

Get up, Miguel! Don't give up on me now! Not when we're so close. *¡Eres un gran covarde! No lo puedo creer.* You are such a coward!

Listen to me, Miguel. Have you forgotten what they did to my father? And to your own sister?! They are corrupt animals, and they're not going to stop.

This rain will not last much longer , and the patrols will return. *Por favor, Miguel, te estoy rogando:* I'm begging you. Take me to the free world. I don't want to go alone. . . . but I will.

Time for a change.

Drama.

Best suited for: **Male, 20 to 30's.**

Sometimes it strikes you. It's a shame, maybe, but we've all got to grow up. Maybe it's been on your mind for quite a while, and you're looking for something more. Although this proclamation is perhaps mainly to make a commitment to yourself, don't overlook the possibility of getting your friend to come along.

How many times have we been here, Tony? A Thousand? Two Thousand? We've been coming to this club almost every day after work since we graduated from high school. We've got our own seats, for cryin' out loud! We're the kings of this place. We're puttin' Mr. Dako's kids through college with all the beers we buy here.

You know what? I'm about to say something profound here, Tony, and I want you to look at me so you know I'm serious. Are you ready? Okay, here it goes. This....is my last beer. I don't mean that this is the last beer I'm having <u>today.</u> And I don't mean that I'm gonna start drinking something else. I mean I'm quitting. I'm gonna change my life. I'm turning over a new leaf. No more drinking, no more wasting time. I'm going down to the Air Force recruiter's office tomorrow. I heard they're looking for mechanics, and that's me. They're offering travel, excitement and an opportunity to move up. You should think about it, too. Take all the time you need, Tony, I still got about half-a-beer left.

The toughest thing.

Drama.

Best suited for: **Female, late 20's and up.**

To maximize the drama and the grief in this monologue, play it "up." Don't let yourself fall into the trap of playing a gloomy piece with lots of gloom. The more casually and more optimistic you play it, the more the viewer will feel the bittersweet pain of losing a loved one. Give your audience that "golf-ball-in-the-throat" feeling by staying very positive. Perhaps you are sharing this with someone in a similar situation who has recently found out about her own mortality.

The toughest thing about finding out that I had terminal cancer, was telling my husband. I just wanted to enjoy every minute that I had left with him. Go to Hawaii, just the two of us, and have some fun. But he had to know.

First, I had to go through the "do-it-yourself" course with him. You know, preparing him for stuff around the house. That brought it all home. Made it real. I never saw a man cry so hard as when I showed him how to run the washing machine. I showed him how I trick our daughter Mary into taking her medicine.

The past few weeks have been so amazing. Paul never knew about my little housewife tricks. Now he even knows where I hide the cookies, which is maybe not such a good thing. I think we fell in love all over again. I now feel confident in turning over the house and parenting completely to him. Tomorrow, we are going to Hawaii....just the two of us.

VFW.

Drama.

Best suited for: **Male or female, late teens and up.**

Rueben could be your brother. You really care about him, and you want him to be with Anna. Get it through to her that Rueben is a great guy. Stick up for him. If she doesn't understand this, then they'll never be together.

Sit down, Anna. I've got to explain something to you, because if you don't understand this, then you don't know Rueben. Rueben is a Veteran of a Foreign War. That's what VFW stands for. And you're right, he often does lose his patience with old people, but not those guys. He's got a lot in common with those old guys at the VFW hall. They've all seen heavy combat. They've all had their lives threatened and had to take the lives of others. That changes a person, and the experience bonds men together even if they fought years apart in different wars. I hear it's kinda like that for women who have had babies. They feel a sisterhood because they understand each other's experience.

Stick with it, Anna. Rueben can be a tough person to get to know and he's a real bear when he wants to be. But you're his type. You're a fighter. Show him you're in this for the long haul. He'll let you inside. And you'll never meet a more loyal, more faithful man than Rueben. He'd lay down his life for you.

You're going to pay.

Drama.

Best suited for: **Male (possibly female), 20's and up.**

Try keeping it calm and in control. Seated if possible. If you can get Michael to pay up through fear and intimidation, you may not have to resort to any rough stuff, so do your best to show him that you mean business.

You look surprised to see me, Michael. Like you didn't expect to see me. Or perhaps there is someplace else you'd rather be, or maybe someone else you'd rather be with. Is that it?

Look at me, Michael. Look at me. I trusted you. I really trusted you. But it turns out you were not the right person to trust. Unfortunately, I learned that the hard way. But don't think you're going to get away with this. You're going to pay, Michael. You're going to pay in full. No discounts. No credit. No monthly deposits. The price is due in full, and it's due now. Anything that you can't pay in cash, you will pay in flesh. Now. . . let's do business, Michael.

You're gonna love these.

Drama.

Best suited for: **Male or female, 20's or younger. (Possibly older.)**

Finally, another chance to play a real "bad guy"! This character is a "low-life", but is very smart and well-spoken. Think Hannibal Lector from "Silence of the Lambs." Intelligence can add to the scariness of the scene by adding to the power of the villain. Your power in this moment comes from your popularity. The scene becomes more creepy the more you calmly explain the obvious benefits, and making the taking of the drugs seem completely harmless.

The problem, you see, is one of perception. Image. How can my friends consider letting you hang out with us if you are unwilling to try something that we all know is a good thing and perfectly safe?

It's a matter of trust and acceptance. You can see that, can't you? If you want to establish rapport with them, then be like them. Show them some similarities. A gesture of commonality. Then, once you are accepted, you can celebrate your differences, and they will appreciate those differences. You see? It's not hard at all. I think you are going to do just great.

Now here. Here's six pills. There's no charge for these. They're on me. Take two of them now, and save the rest for later. You're gonna love these. Go ahead, take two of 'em, and I'll go let the others know that you're ready to hang out with us.

You've never been there for me, Dad.

Drama.

Best suited for: **Male, 20-40.**

This monologue doesn't need a lot of explanation. The power is in its confrontational manner. Keep in mind that a strong choice might be that this son may not be trying to hurt his father for the sake of revenge, rather, using guilt to get him to change. You may, therefore, choose to play with how much anger is behind this. Play with a palette of vulnerability and hope, but go headlong into that uncomfortable confrontation.

No, Dad, you listen to me. Did you even know that I used to play baseball? I'd be surprised if you did 'cause you never came to a single one of my games. Everyone else had a mom or dad who would show up at the games. I was good, too. But there was never anyone there that I cared about to tell me, "Good job." And no one was there to pat me on the back and cheer me up when I struck out. You were never there! Not for baseball. Not for homework. Not for Boy Scouts. You were too busy working.

So I guess it shouldn't upset me so much that you're not planning to attend my wedding. I guess I should be used to it. But it does upset me, Dad. In fact, it upsets me a lot. And it's going to upset Karen, too. You have to change. And you have to make that change now. If you want to be able to spend time with me and your future daughter-in-law, and your future grandkids, think about it... And make it to that wedding.

Acronymble.

Comedy.

Best suited for: **Male or female, late teens and up.**

Tough to memorize, not much to show off true acting skill, but it can be very funny, and it always holds their attention. Enjoy.

Last week, my friend T.J. and I took a TWA flight from SFO back home to LAX, and drove to his HQ in his Hum-V while listening to a U2 CD on his JVC. Now, I think U2 is OK, but I could listen to AC/DC 24/7. The next day TJ's Hum-V was SOL, so we took my VW. It's fast. A GT. So we took the I-5 to the PCH to see my other friend, J.R. He's smart. He's a CPA. He's got a B.S. from UCLA and an MBA from MIT. We watched an episode of E.R. on his TV, then a tape of WKRP on his VCR. Then we all got in my VW. (You see, J.R. can't drive right now, because he drove his BMW while drinking J.D. and got a DUI and now has to go to AA.) Anyway, we went to lunch. I had a BLT and a glass of OJ. On the way home from lunch, we listened to NPR, and the DJ said that the FBI had put out an APB on a guy who'd been selling 8x10's of US ICBM's to the former USSR, and his ID matched J.R. to a tee! So T.J. and I looked at each other, and then we slowly turned and looked at J.R. We were just joking, but he freaked, and even though I was driving 60 on southbound 101, he leaped out of my VW PDQ! Needless to say, he needed a lot of TLC. When the EMT's arrived, they put on gloves to prevent TB, HIV, and a variety of other STD's. Then they took him to the ER ASAP. At first, they thought he was DOA, but the Doc had a high IQ. (He got his Ph.D. and MD from NYU, and he got a 4.0 GPA.) So he hooked up an EKG and said that J.R. would be A-OK. But the procedure wasn't covered by his HMO, and we had no cash, so T.J. and I had to drive around at 11:30 pm looking for an ATM. We finally found a B of A, but there were two huge SOB's standing around looking very suspicious. One looked like he was ex-USMC and the other, a lineman for the NFL. They turned out just to be a TV crew for ABC shooting a special for 20/20 about another S & L scandal, and they were happy because they were making lots of OT. PS, the Doc got thirsty and reached for a glass of H20, but it was H2SO4. Ouch. J.R. is fine, and decided to join the ACLU. T.J. now plays for the PGA, and me? I just sit around and think up a bunch of BS using my ABC's!

But I *am* mature!

Comedy.

Best suited for: Male or female, teens and up.

A good choice for showing range. A strong and romantic, serious tone at the beginning sets up a comedic ending. Have fun getting your audience ready for the unexpected. The names have been selected here to keep it non-specific with regard to sex.

I don't get it, Chris. I just don't get it. What we had was so wonderful. So special. We had the kind of relationship that most people only dream of. I always pictured us as Romeo and Juliet. I loved you that much. And now, you want to end it all, saying that I'm not mature enough. Not mature enough? I'm sorry, I just don't see it. Not mature enough!! I don't quite know how to respond to that, except to say, I'm rubber and you're glue and anything you say bounces off me and sticks to you!

Wait, I'm sorry. I know that I shouldn't have said that. It's just that I get rather stressed and upset when you make remarks like that. I've tried to make myself clear about that but still you call me names. Well you're not the boss of me, and I think you're just a big, fat, poo-poo, ca-ca head!

Cindi, with an "i".

Comedi. (sorry)

Best suited for: **Female, late 20's and up.**

The trick to this monologue is in creating a believable transition from sad and hurt, to angry and devious in a short phone conversation. As with other pieces written for the telephone, you may choose to make this a face-to-face meeting.

Carol? . . .Hi, it's Bev.
. . .Great. I've just had a l[o]
like to talk . . .Well, okay, B[i]
an affair. But I can't get my
He's my big snuggle bear. . . [I]
been bowling a lot lately sin[ce]   [betw]een
jobs again, and I was doing t[he] [l]aundry and
found a name and phone number on a piece
of paper. "Cindi," with an "i." And the "i"
didn't just have a dot over it, it had a little
heart, I swear to God.

Then, when I looked in the medicine
cabinet, right there, between his foot-odor
powder and his hair-replacement foam, I
found cologne. "Love Hunk." And it was new,
too, 'cause he's never worn cologne or
deodorant or anything since I've known him.
And then, when I was bringing him a beer
during the football game, I accidentally
spilled some on his recliner chair, and while
he was yelling at me, he slipped and called
me Cindi.

(She is suddenly hearing her own
words.)

You know what? I guess I can leave
him. You know what else? I've still got that
fat, bald, stinking, out-of-work bastard's
credit card. Carol? Let's go to Hawaii for a
few weeks. I suddenly feel so much better!

105

The
(fill in the blank)
Foundation

Comedy.

Best suited for: **Male or female, any age.**

As with any comedy piece, if you get it, you can probably do it. If you don't see the humor, move on to the next. Just have fun with this one. This can be done as if to a live audience, or as a Public Service Announcement. Make it seem as realistic and sincere as possible. Put your name in the blanks, or make up a character name.

Hi. My name is _____, and I'm here to introduce you to something that has become very important to me over the years. It's an opportunity to give, to show you care, and to make a difference in someone else's life. I'm speaking of course about the _____ Foundation.

When you give to the _____ Foundation, there are no commissions or administrative fees, so you can be assured that 100% of your contribution will go directly where it's needed. To me, _____.

The spirit of giving is something that we all need to feel. We all know that there are starving children and endangered species around the world, and many of you have donated generously to those worthy causes. But we've got some issues right here at home that we need to take care of, too. The Mercedes that I purchased with your previous generous donations is now almost two years old, and the air conditioning system isn't as cold as it used to be. And think about all those servants who work for me, both here at my home as well as on board my yacht. Don't you think that they deserve a raise? Of course you do!

So please, get out your checkbook or credit card, and call now. The _____ Foundation. Working together, we really can make a difference.

The funniest thing just happened.

Comedy.

Best suited for: **Male, 20's and up.**

Break the news to her as sweetly as possible. It's a no-win situation, so you are "walking on egg shells". It might be fun to try to get her to laugh, even though your opening lines will probably make her very suspicious.

Honey? Sweetie? Sugar Muffin? The funniest thing just happened! I was just downstairs in the casino. Do you remember that sheik who bought us the champagne at dinner? Well, he invited me to join his private poker game. You are not going to believe this. I was dealt three aces, so I bet everything I had, and drew two queens! Boom! A full house! The bidding kept going up, but I wanted to stay in the game and buy you that new station wagon you've been hinting about.

So, the sheik, he's really a nice man by the way, he drops a straight flush, ten high, on the table just as calm as you please. Boom! Just like that! I was thoroughly impressed. The guy has class.

Anyway, here's the funny part. You're gonna laugh. Honey . . . it's only for a year . . . but your last name is going to be Baharambanakazul. Isn't that funny? Baharambanakazul. I laughed when he pronounced it for me. Sweetie, his men are waiting for you outside, but I promise you . . . When you are done being one of his wives for a year . . . I'm gonna be waiting for you, Sugar Dumpling. And there's gonna be a new station wagon waitin' in the driveway, too.

Grindlemeyer Wineries.

Comedy.

Best suited for: **Male or female, late teens and up.**

This is a piece that reflects the humor in the British television comedies of the 70's. Play it sincerely. You can experiment with accents if you are so inclined.

I won!

Comedy.

Best suited for: **Male or female, any age.**

Here is a very specific monologue. Yes, it can be done by anyone, but only in a very few circumstances. An example might be a monologue competition where your name (or competition number) is to be called out when it's your turn to start. If that's the case, this one might work well. Trick them into believing your excitement, and you'll get them to feel something in the short time that you are given to work with. Begin your response immediately once your name is called.

Grindlemeyer Wineries, how may I help you? . . . Oh, you're not satisfied with your purchase? Well we will be happy to provide you with a full refund or exchange if you'll just answer a few questions for us. What wine did you buy from us? Mm-h m. And was that the premium or regular label? Regular? Okay. And your complaint is . . . It didn't taste good. Well, Sir, perhaps you can be more specific. Was it too sweet, or dry, or fruity, or too woody, or syrupy, or honeyed?.....Oh, too dry. Do you mean dry in a vacuous, barren, and superficial way, or more of a tangy, acerbic, rancid or tart way? . . . Tangy? What kind of tangy? Was it biting, or piercing, caustic or sharp, or did you find it to be more of an intense, fleshy, overcast, solicitous brine? Or even a swarthy, aromatic, emanating, distinctly floral, obstinate and confused native bitterness guilded in complete arcane alkalinity?.....Oh, it just wasn't full-bodied you say. Does that mean that you found it to be a bit thin, or lean, or gaunt, or svelte, or coolly emaciated, or openly lanky? Or perhaps you merely found it sad and despondent with a bouquet of cautious overtones veiled by a pensive emanation of doleful melancholy. . . Oh, okay, all right. Now we're getting down to it. You really just don't like the container. Well you know, Sir, you can take the plastic foil pouch out of the cardboard box. That will change the look a lot. They're just harder to stack that way.

I don't just fix 'em.

Drama or **Comedy**.

Best suited for: **Male, 20 and up**.

It doesn't matter whether or not this guy's story is true, we tend to believe it because it's so filled with detail. Keep him likable, and work to impress Mr. Jordan and get this job. Regional accents might work well with this piece, but so might a straight, crisp all-American guy next door. This monologue is light, and depending on how you choose to perform it, it can range anywhere from serious to hilarious.

Fix 'em? No, Mr. Jordan, I do more than just fix 'em. When I'm wor it's not just an automobile. It's a car! Wl was little, I never wanted to play with t Not even toy cars. Even as a toddler parents usually found me getting all grea under one of the family cars. Drove mother crazy thinking I'd get run over, but think my dad was kinda proud. When reached that time in my life when I no longe needed a diaper change, I could already do an oil change. My folks always had cheap cars so I got lots of practice. At five years old I did a complete tune-up. At six years old I changed a water pump. Seven, replaced a master cylinder. Eight, ground my first transmission flywheel, and at nine years old, I did a complete rebuild on a small-block Chevy 302, all by myself. I was a child prodigy! The local paper did a big article about me. I've still got it if you'd like to see it.

Mr. Jordan, I'm like a wild animal trainer. I can make 'em purr. Or if you want, I can make 'em growl. I talk to the cars. I listen to 'em. I understand 'em. They trust me.

Now I know I charge more for my services that the other mechanics, Mr. Jordan. But I do a lot more than just fix 'em.

That's me! I won! Oh my gosh, this is so exciting. I never win anything! I'm just so happy that I can hardly catch my breath. Uh, I'd like to thank my acting coach, and my director. I'd like to thank my parents and all that they have done for me. And I'd like to thank God, for giving me the skills and motivation to keep at it until I finally won. Wow, I'm so excited I'm about to pee my pants.

Okay, so what did I win? A car? A vacation? Cash? (Look over at timekeeper's/event coordinator's podium.) Is that the list of prizes? Come on, let's see. (Go to see list.) Well. . . wait a sec. . . this is just the list to tell who goes next for the monologues. . . You mean, I didn't win anything?. . . . You just called out my name because it was my turn to do my monologue?. . . Oh. . . well. . . I don't have enough time now!

See, I told you I never win anything.

Speeding?   Me?

Comedy.

Best suited for: **Male or female, any age old enough to drive.**

Reminiscent of television sit-coms, this piece finds its humor in its rambling dialogue. The "add-on" patterns of speech appear loose, but must be precisely timed.   To give the viewer a greater sense to speaking to a cop, stay seated, and speak to your left, as though out the driver's window.   If on stage, turn the chair sideways facing stage right, so that you can be seen and heard by your audience.

Speeding? Me? You think I was speeding? In this piece of junk? Officer, I don't think this car could exceed the speed limit even if I floored it. Not even if I floored it down a steep hill. Not even if I floored it down a steep hill with a strong tailwind. It's just not happening. Not in this baby, no Sir. Besides, I'm a cautious and careful driver. Always have been. Nosebleeds. If I accelerate too fast, I get nosebleeds. It's not pretty. My friends even tease me because they say I drive like an old lady.

Uh, Sir, I see you're still writing. You know, the thing is that I'm sorry, you see. That's the thing. And I've never gotten a ticket before, so perhaps this time, you can just give me a warning. Maybe a really, really strong warning. You could slap my face and call me some very bad names and I'd be so warned I'm sure I'd never speed again. Maybe that's an idea. Huh?

Okay, okay, okay. I can see you're a man of integrity. You've got a job that you take seriously and I think that's great. Really. Integrity is a very noble trait. The world needs more people like you. But let me ask you this, isn't forgiveness a noble trait, too?

Stewardess Rap.

Comedy.

Best suited for: Male or Female, any age.

A "stand-up comedy" approach is recommended with this one, speaking directly to your audience, although you may work out another way to set up this piece. You've got to be able to completely let go with this one, and get into the part, or it won't fly. Set up the rap with a little "boom-box beat".

Whenever I fly, I'm always so impressed with the stewardess'. They always look so classy and refined, no matter what the circumstances. But on my flight last week, we had this stewardess that redefines what being a stewardess is all about. She was wild! I swear, she was someone who was working in a field other than what she was born for. I'll tell you what she said, and you tell me if you think I'm right.

I'm your Rappin' Stewardess,
Jeanette is my name,
Please notice all the exits,
On both sides of the plane.

Keep your seatbelts on,
'Cause our descent is mighty steep,
And if you press that service button,
I'll kick you in the "beeeep".

Don't mess with me up here,
I warn you cause I mean it,
You want your little snack,
But I'm the Queen of the Peanut.

I thought I'd be a stewardess,
Because I like to fly,
But now I just stand by the door,
Saying, "Bu-bye, Mm-Hm, Bu-Bye".

There's nothing worse.

Comedy.

Best suited for: **Male or female, any age.**

This one is probably best performed as a stand-up routine, meaning that you are speaking directly to the audience, using a microphone if possible. When doing stand-up, you are usually not acting as a character as much as you are playing yourself, relating personal experiences. As off-the-wall as this piece is, make us believe at the beginning that you really are uncomfortable up on stage. (For many performers, that's no problem!) Have fun.

Hi. Man it's tough being up here. It's hard, you know? I really don't enjoy this at all. I can't even figure out why I agreed to get up here because I really can't think of anything worse. There is nothing worse than this.

Well, okay, if you were strapped into a chair while an evil dentist drilled open all your teeth without Novocain and stuck ice on them while a North Vietnamese prison camp warden pulled out your toenails with a pair of pliers. I guess that would be worse.

Or. . . if you were playing around with a scalpel and accidentally cut open your chest cavity from sternum to navel and all of your guts and heart and lungs and everything spilled out onto the street and then a big truck came by and squashed over your guts and then part of your small intestine got caught in the axle of the truck and it started dragging you, and you got dragged fourteen miles because the driver had Country Classics 102.7 cranked up on the truck radio hauling a load of sugar beets to Stockton. That would be worse.

Or. . . if you were home alone at night on Friday the 13th and there's thunder and lightning and then you hear a mysterious knock on the door, and you open it and. . . it's Barney! That big purple dinosaur guy! Oooh!

Hmm. So maybe being up here isn't really so bad.

Treat her right.

Comedy.

Best suited for: **Male, teens and up.**

You believe in your approach toward impressing women. Let Dave know that you are serious. He's lucky to have a friend like you with such wisdom and experience.

Dave, I know you're nervous about this first date with Lorri, but if you follow my advice, you can't lose. If you're willing to put out that extra effort to make it really special, there's no way that she won't fall for you. Follow my plan, and it's virtually guaranteed. I went on a first date with a girl a few nights ago and she was absolutely blown away.

Her name was Beth. She had mentioned that she liked the old Tarzan movies, so I showed up for the date dressed in nothing but a leather loincloth. I think that right away, she knew that this was going to be a special night. Also, I didn't want her to feel awkward during those uncomfortable moments of silence that sometimes occur on a first date, so I just kept talking non-stop the whole night so that she could relax.

I reached over and cut her food for her and she didn't even ask me to.

Her glass of red wine had a bit of cork floating in it, and I wanted to show her that I would stick up for her and be on her side, so I stood up on the table and screamed across the room to the waiter, "You call this service?"! Then I hurled the glass over the other tables and hit the waiter right in the head. It was a great throw, you should have seen it. I think that kind of impressed her.

And then, at the end of dinner, against all of my natural impulses and my old-fashioned training, I gave her the opportunity to be a modern woman by insisting that she pay the bill.

At this point, I know things were going great. She didn't even know what to say. She must have been very moved. She just sat there and cried. It was beautiful.

No, Dave, girls just aren't prepared for it when a guy knows how to treat her right.

123

Wizzin' off a bridge.

Comedy.

Best suited for: Male, any age.

Let's admit it guys, there are only a few things that we can really do better than girls, so let's celebrate our limited advantages. Have fun with this piece by really doing everything you can to get your best friend out of the dumps.

You're down right now, sure. Women. I've seen this before. I'm tellin' ya Jeremy, you need to express your deepest calling as a man. You need to get Karen out of your mind, and to do that, you've got to embrace your complete manliness. Tonight, we celebrate our distinctive status as MEN!

Now I'm not talking about the little stuff. The stuff that's merely "inclined" toward men, like football or dark beer. And I'm not talking about the middle-kinda stuff that most women just don't appreciate, like black licorice or the Three Stooges.

No, Jeremy. I'm talking about that one special action that God clearly intended only for men to enjoy . . . Wizzin' off a bridge. Trust me, Jeremy. Get over to that bridge and let it fly! Do it now! You'll forget about Karen, . . . and you'll be closer to God.

J.P. Pierce lives, writes, teaches and makes movies and stuff in the Los Angeles area. You can contact him by email: impactfilms@jps.net

Now, get out there and kill 'em with your monologue!

"Killer Monologues" on Video!

This breakthrough method of acting instruction brings you J.P. Pierce personally coaching you on monologue performance. Use this easy-to-follow visual guide, along with the book, to get the most comprehensive training available on monologues. Watch first-hand as acting students like you perform many of the monologues found in this book. Order the video and supercharge your progress!

Killer Monologues (book) $14.95

Killer Monologues (video)..$29.95

Killer Monologues (book & video combo) $39.95

Shipping and handling per book, video, or combo $2.50

California residents add sales tax 8.25%
($1.23 per book, $2.47 per video, $3.29 per combo)

Rush orders are available at an additional cost.

Call, write or email your request to:
IMPACT FILMS
14431 Ventura Blvd., Suite 248
Sherman Oaks, CA 91423

Call: **818-994-7888**
email: impactfilms@jps.net

It's better to be making the news than taking it;
to be an actor rather than a critic.

- Winston Churchill (1874-1965)